LEADERTHINK ®

Inspiring Reminders to Think – and Act – Like a Leader

Volume Two

Tracy Brown

Dallas, Texas
2009

LeaderThink®
Inspiring Reminders to Think – and Act – Like a Leader
Volume 2
By Tracy Brown

ISBN-13: 978-1-889819-25-9

Cover design by www.kbiDesigns.com
Author Photo: Jim Duncan, www.DuncanPhotography.com

brown bridges books
PO Box 12866
Dallas TX 75225

Dedication

To everyone with a desire to lead

You can be a leader for the 21st century
at work
at school
in your family
in your community
on your athletic team
in your professional association
in your spiritual community
in your city or state
in your choir or band
in your profession
You can be a leader for the 21st century
It's up to you!

Other Books by This Author

Author:

LeaderThink®: Inspiring Reminders to Think – and Act – Like a Leader, Volume 1

Breaking the Barrier of Bias: The Subtle Influence of Bias and What to Do About It.

71 Ways to Demonstrate Commitment to Diversity

motiVersity: Motivating While Valuing Diversity

Diagnosis Diversity: How to Maximize Diversity in Healthcare Settings

Contributing Author:

The Productivity Path: Your Roadmap for Improving Employee Performance!

The Leadership Path: Your Roadmap for Leading People in the 21st Century!

The Service Path: Your Roadmap for Building Strong Customer Loyalty!

Affiliated Websites

www.TheWayLeadersThink.com
www.DiversityTrends.com
www.TracyBrown.com
www.DiagnosisDiversity.com
www.DiversityResourcesonSale.com
www.DiversityAwarenessWeek.com

LeaderThink®

Inspiring Reminders to Think – and Act – Like a Leader

Hopefully you read LeaderThink® Volume 1 and are back for more encouragement, more empowerment and more engaging quotations.

The format is the same as in Volume 1. Each article begins with a quotation that is followed by a brief commentary.

The quotations are words of wisdom from a wide variety of people representing diversity in age, ethnicity, national origin, culture, gender, sexual identity and religion. Each quotation is different but the message is the same: Leadership requires a certain mindset and a commitment to action.

But maybe this book is your first introduction to LeaderThink®. If that's the case, then let me welcome you!

The LeaderThink® books give you the opportunity to read and enjoy messages from the weekly LeaderThink® email newsletter that were published in the past.

There are (at least) three ways to use this book.

1. You can read this book in sequence.

2. You can scan the Table of Contents to find a quote that interests you then go to the corresponding page and read the commentary related to the quotation you selected.

3. Many people simply open the book to a random page and see what ideas or insights are there.

This book won't magically turn you into the best leader in the world. But it will provide bite-size reminders (you can read in five minutes or less) to think, and act, like a leader!

Table of Contents

LeaderThink® Volume 2

Inspiring Reminders to Think – and Act – Like a Leader

"People who make a living doing something they don't enjoy wouldn't even be happy with a one-day work week."
Duke Ellington

Are you making a living, or making a life? Do you love what you do to make a living?

When you have a passion for what you do, you love going to work each day.

When you enjoy what you do, it is much easier to deal with the challenges that are a part of every job.

As a leader, it becomes much easier to encourage others when you are doing something you like to do and when you work in an organization you believe in.

Think . . . and act . . . like a leader!

"The ultimate measure of a man is not where he stands in moments of comfort and convenience, but where he stands at times of challenge and controversy."

Martin Luther King Jr.

As a leader, what do you do when the going gets rough? How do you handle it when things are not going smoothly? When there are unexpected downturns in the market or a large contract gets cancelled are you at your best as a leader?

None of us wants every day to be full of challenge or controversy. But I believe the true test of a leader is what he does when all the cards seem stacked against him.

In good times it's easy to accept the responsibilities of leadership. But in challenging times the spotlight is on you to make decisions that further the mission and culture of the organization. In challenging times it is the leader who must communicate, communicate and communicate more to keep both internal and external stakeholders engaged.

Think . . . and act . . . like a leader!

"I always had something to shoot for each year: to jump one inch farther."

Jackie Joyner Kersee

What will you do to be "one inch farther" as a leader this year?

Please don't make a long list of New Year resolutions. Don't promise your family and friends a dozen things you will do (or not do) in the coming months. And do not go into work and share a list of all the ways you are going to be a better leader this year.
Instead, try this.

Choose one thing. Choose one behavior you want to work on and list 12 ways you will work on that one thing.

Then go to your calendar, planner or PDA and write one of those 12 ways in each month.

Do not share your list of 12 tactics with anyone; although you should feel free to share the one behavior you are committing to work on. You might even ask a few people to give you feedback throughout the year on how you are doing.

But mostly you will hold yourself accountable. Each month when you look at your calendar you will see the reminder for what you are going to apply.

By the end of the year you will be "one inch farther" toward your go as of being a great leader.

Happy New Year! And don't forget to . . . .

Think . . . and act . . . like a leader!

"To get where you want to go you can't only do what you like."

Peter Abrahams

Whenever we start a new year, or a new project, or a new job, we get so excited.

We think about all the things we WANT to do to make it work.

We envision all the FUN ways we can showcase our talent or our creativity.

We know it might take some HARD WORK, but we downplay that part of the equation.

Newsflash: the hard work, the discipline, the doing what needs to be done . . . that is all a part of achieving the goal.

As a leader you don't have the luxury of only doing what you want to do. You have the responsibility to do what needs to be done.

If you are lucky, much of what has to be done excites, energizes and enriches you. But if you need to do some things that depress and disgust you too, remember it's all a part of the job.

Great leaders do what they like - and what they don't like – to achieve their goals.

Think . . . and act . . . like a leader!

"When a person goes against his values in the choices he makes, the failure is automatic."
Howard Thurman

If you are in a job that goes against your values find a new job.

If you are serving on a Board of Directors for an organization that requires you to work with people in ways that don't align with your values, resign from that Board immediately.

You can not lead people where you don't want them to go.

I once served on a Board where everyone talked about inclusion, about being respectful and about changing the status quo. I was excited about joining this Board for those very reasons. I wanted to be a part of continuing the important mission of this group while growing it to be more representative of the community and helping the leadership learn to deal with diversity of thought, style and ethnicity.

The first year went great. I was learning about the group and its leaders; they were learning about me.

The second year was difficult; I began challenging the fact that we were saying one thing and doing another.

The third year became unbearable; I began to be viewed as difficult and uncooperative. I began to view the organization as hypocritical and fearful of what they said they most wanted.

Ultimately I resigned.

By contrast, I am a part of another organization where my values about communication, honesty, leadership and innovation are all in perfect alignment with the leadership and values of the association. As individuals we don't always agree about strategy or tactics, but we are operating from the same values so we are usually able to resolve issues with the best interest of the organization in mind.

What about you? Do you work (or volunteer) in places where your values help you succeed? If not, choose a different path.

Think . . . and act . . . like a leader!

"There are no unimportant people and there are no insignificant events."

Tracy Brown

Do you know the name of the janitor?

When you call or visit other managers do you actually speak to their assistants and acknowledge them?

Can you name the daughters or the church or the hobbies of your most recent new hire or addition to the board?

You have a busy schedule to maintain. But are you really too busy to see and respect the people you encounter as you accomplish the business of your department or board? Are you really too busy to let the people you come into contact with know you recognize their contribution - not only to your success, but also their contribution to the world?

Do you believe you are too important to bother with being nice to the doorman who greets you with a smile or the busboy who clears the dishes so you can enjoy your dessert?

Great leaders are never too busy to look each person in the eye with genuine concern. Great leaders grab every opportunity to let people know how much they matter.

Great leaders don't pretend to care; they do care and it shows in all they do.

Think . . . and act . . . like a leader!

"If you're going to bring about change, do it and be done with it."
Melvin Chapman

The essence of change is this: Decide. Act. Repeat.

DECIDE
If you were to decide to carry the spirit of Hanukkah, Christmas, or Kwanzaa into every day, week or month of your life would it make a positive difference? Would it make you a better person? Would it make you a better leader?

ACT
Whether you have a personal connection to any of those religious and cultural celebrations or not, think about what you appreciate most about the winter holiday season. Use that insight to change your world. Use that insight to help yourself, and others, to be as generous as possible throughout the year.

Maybe you want to focus on forgiveness. Or tolerance. Or sharing. Or family. Or gratitude. Whatever positive emotion or behavior that seems to be most apparent to you during this time of year – begin to incorporate it into your life week after week.

REPEAT

The quote above says, "do it and be done with it" but I don't think it means to do something just one time. I interpret it to mean stop thinking about what you are going to do and just do it. Do it again. Then do it some more. Do it consistently and intentionally rather than thinking, dreaming or talking about it.

Let the holiday season guide you to what values and behaviors are most important for you to demonstrate as a leader. Then be done with the talking. Be done with the thinking. Be done with the dreaming.

Great leaders are great change agents; and the biggest changes begin within.

Think . . . and act . . . like a leader!

"Do the one thing you think you cannot do. Fail at it. Try again. Do better the second time. The only people who never tumble are those who never mount the high wire. This is your moment. Own it."
Oprah Winfrey

January is the month we set our intentions for the year. Are you committed to trying something new? Is one of your goals for this year to improve your knowledge or your work performance? Maybe you have goals to lead your department or team to better results and stronger relationships.

If you are hoping to excel as a leader, or in any other aspect of your life, you must be prepared to fail and keep going.

Great leaders are not perfect. They are persistent.

Great leaders don't know everything. They know how to use everything others know.

Great leaders are not fearless. They just fear change less than others.

Great leaders may not be the smartest person in the group. They are simply smart enough to tap into the experience and ideas of every group member in a way that helps everyone achieve more.

You can be a great leader. All it takes is a little patience, persistence, courage, creativity and commitment.

Think . . . and act . . . like a leader!

> *"We often give up and blame our lack of progress on not having the most up to date tools. (But) The Grand Canyon was carved with water."*

Patrick J McBride

Have you recently heard any of the excuses below? Or worse, have you recently USED any of the statements below?

- We don't have the latest technology.
- We don't have enough staff.
- We don't have the smartest people.
- We don't have a committed CEO.
- We don't have enough data.
- We don't have a strong team.
- We don't have state of the art equipment.

You can always want more, better, faster, smarter people. You can always plan for a time when you can staff your organization differently. But for now . . .

Don't let what you DON'T have be an excuse that keeps you from achieving the best possible result with what you DO have!

Great leaders unleash the talent and creativity of the people they have to meet (or exceed) the expectations of others.

Think . . . and act . . . like a leader!

"It is important for meeting leaders to know the difference between the process of the meeting and the content of the meeting."

Fran Rees

What your meeting is about is the content. How your meeting runs is the process. The success of your meeting depends on how well you match the process you use with the content being discussed in order to achieve your desired goal.

I recently attended a meeting where the primary goal was to insure members of a newly chartered project team understood their responsibilities so they could work without direct supervision.

The manager who planned the meeting felt it was a great success but during the next 8 weeks he was frustrated by the constant questions and emails he received from team members. He kept saying, "We covered that in the meeting." or "Why don't they go look in their notebook from the meeting?"

Clearly the content of the meeting had all the information; so I asked him about the process used during the meeting. He described an agenda that involved a series of expert presenters from 9am to 4pm with a break during lunch. And during lunch most participants spent 30 minutes checking email and returning phone calls.

This was a great example of paying so much attention to content that the process was almost ignored.

A better process for this meeting would have been to start during the weeks before the meeting soliciting questions from the team members about what they needed to know. Then, speakers could address specific questions members of the group were thinking about. The number of speakers could have been cut in half and a significant part of the day should have included team members working in subgroups to explore how they planned to apply the information being shared by the experts who were providing formal presentation. Through this kind of process, team members would be connecting the knowledge with future actions; their questions would have been raised (and answered) right away.

Think as much about what process will give you the results you want as you think about what content will provide the information you need to deliver. Great leaders balance process and content – even in a brief one-on-one meeting with subordinates or peers.

Think . . . and act . . . like a leader!

"An inch of progress is worth more than a yard of complaint."

Booker T Washington

If you are like me it is sometimes hard for you to celebrate small progress. It is much easier to stay focused on the end goal and to work at a feverish pitch until you reach that goal.

One thing I have learned about only viewing success as reaching the end goal is that we forget to celebrate the small accomplishments. And realistically, it is the small accomplishments stacked upon each other that create the stairway to final success.

So, this week, stop and celebrate each inch of progress. Don't complain about what has not yet been completed. Stop focusing on the disappointments and failures you may have observed or experienced. Replace your irritation about delays with some genuine appreciation for deeds accomplished.

Try it . . . and see if it makes a difference!

Think . . . and act . . . like a leader!

"Creativity can solve almost any problem. The creative act, the defeat of habit by originality, overcomes everything."

George Lois

This definition of creativity - an act that defeats a habit – is intriguing to me.

Too often we equate "creativity" with the word "artistic." We commonly think if someone is "creative" they have ideas or approaches no one else could come up with. But in reality, any time we break away from the old ways of doing things we are being creative.

We are creating a different approach or learning to practice a different response every time we stop doing things the way we've always done them or stop reacting to people the way we have always reacted.

And I hope you agree with me that it takes a spark of creativity to even be WILLING to try something new. Great leaders nourish the creativity of their peers and followers.

Think . . . and act . . . like a leader!

"Don't let one closed door stop you."
Terrie Michelle Williams

How many times have you been tempted to just stop? You felt defeated. Someone else was chosen for the job you wanted. Or perhaps you weren't selected to represent your department on a high-visibility project. Maybe the proposal you worked on for the last 4 weeks was simply not approved.

It is not a good feeling when the door to your next major success closes. It leaves you wondering what your next step should be. And sometimes it is very difficult to keep going.

But great leaders know that closed doors are not the same as closed coffins. Your life is not over. Your team needs you to look ahead and provide direction for next steps.

A closed door just means you should regroup and go knock on the next door.

A closed door simply means 'not now' or 'not this opportunity'.

Don't stand at the closed door so long that you fail to notice when the next door opens.

Shake off your disappointment when doors close and start working on the next goal, the next dream, the next project.

Think . . . and act . . . like a leader!

"Wisdom does not live in only one house."
Ashanti Proverb

This week, notice the wisdom of the people around you. Focus on how you can best utilize the education, experience and expertise of your peers, subordinates and co-workers.

Great leaders encourage others to be at the best. Great leaders create an environment where people can demonstrate excellence by using their own wisdom, passion and creativity.

It is great to be wise . . . but it is even a greater gift to your organization if you are a leader who taps in to the wisdom of all the people on your team.

Think . . . and act . . . like a leader!

"We learn the rope of life by untying its knots."
Jean Toomer

Being a leader can be fun. Leaders get to make decisions, solve problems, build systems, develop people, resolve customer issues, develop new approaches and guide teams of people to achieve great success.

But sometimes, on the way to that great success, we get tied up in a few pitfalls. We procrastinate, we ignore glaring issues, we try to hide our ignorance, and we fail to ask for help.

When issues come up that are like the knots in a rope we just need to slow down and deal with the problem before us. Taking care of it while it is small will help us avoid a larger problem later.

We become more skilled and more confident with each knot we untie. We become better leaders with each problem or challenge we resolve.

Think . . . and act . . . like a leader!

"If you are patient in one moment of anger, you will escape a hundred days of sorrow."

Chinese Proverb

You are under a lot of pressure.

You have one meeting after another all day.

And between two of these meetings you stop by the office of a colleague to pick up the updated report you need for the next meeting.

She's not in her office and you don't see the report on her desk. Her assistant is out sick today and your meeting starts in 15 minutes.

Angry? If you are normal your first reaction is to be angry that this colleague did not have the material you needed ready for you when you needed it. She knew you would be stopping by to pick it up and that you would be on a very tight schedule.

Because it's been such a stressful day already you are thinking of several mean things you might say to her . . . or about her. You grab a post it note and write a short message: Where are you? I need that report! Bring it to Conference Room C as soon as you return."

And since you have an extra 10 minutes you decide to swing by your office just to check on things in your department.

All the way back to your desk you are fuming and thinking about how you will verbally report at the meeting based on the information you can remember from the previous version of the report.

When you arrive at your desk you see the report you were expecting with a note. "I have a family emergency but I know you need this report. Note the changes on pages 8, 15 and 22 and call me on my cell phone if you have any questions. Everything else is as we discussed 3 days ago."

Be patient in your moment of anger . . . or risk making a bad situation worse!

Think . . . and act . . . like a leader!

Twenty years from now you will be more disappointed by the things that you didn't do than by the ones you did do. So throw off the bowlines. Sail away from the safe harbor. Catch the trade winds in your sails."

Mark Twain

What changes are you afraid to make, even though you know they would be good for you or for your organization?

What conversations would you have with peers or subordinates if you weren't so busy being politically correct?

What projects would you tackle if you really believed in your ability to succeed in spite of challenges?

Do you want to look back at some future point and regret the chances you didn't take?

Or will you expand the boundaries you think confine you and go after the best in you, tap into the best in your team and create the best outcomes for your organization?

Great leaders assess the environment, lock their sights on grand achievements and set sail on a journey toward tomorrow's successes.

Think . . . and act . . . like a leader!

"The world is moved along not only by the mighty shoves of its heroes but also by the aggregate of the tiny pushes of each honest worker."

Helen Keller

I bet there have been a few times when you, as a leader, have felt like a hero.

You might have felt like a hero because you brought in new business. Or maybe you were recognized as Member of the Year in your association. Perhaps you developed a new process or program that turned around a struggling department or product.

There are all kinds of ways to become recognized for major change or big shifts that fix an existing problem.

But often, those big changes and visible programs are really small compared to the dozens, or even hundreds, of invisible improvements made by individuals who are never recognized.

Don't forget to notice, and acknowledge, the many people who do the small things that set you up for the big successes.

Great leaders understand they are building big successes on the foundation of tiny bricks silently laid by the every day actions of everyone in the organization.

Think . . . and act . . . like a leader!

"You've got to think about big things while you're doing small things, so that all the small things go in the right direction."

Alvin Toffler

Rushing in and out of meetings. Taking phone calls. Returning email. Solving problems. Giving feedback. Changing deadlines. These are the little things of daily work life.

But as a leader, you can never afford to lose touch with the big goals, the vision for the association or company and the mission you are helping to fulfill.

It's the big things that help you prioritize the small things.

It's the big things that communicate the standards you expect everyone to meet.

It's the big things that the company, the customer and the community see or think about when they are interacting with your organization.

The little things count and create the one-on-one experiences for us all. But we can only claim the title of great leader if those little things are in alignment with the big things our organization stands for!

Think . . . and act . . . like a leader!

"Every day is a donation to eternity and even one hour is a contribution to the future."
King Kheti of Egypt

Great leaders know their smallest decisions can change the future and their tiniest actions have the ability to change lives.

Think back over your the past 24 hours; what did YOU contribute to eternity?

Did your words and actions lay a foundation for success for your department, organization, community or family?

Everything you do gets woven together to create your legacy.

Think . . . and act . . . like a leader!

"The best way to find yourself is to lose yourself in the service of others."

Gandhi

Every day this week ask yourself this question: "What did I do today to help someone else?"

Pay attention to your answers.

Are you helping others achieve THEIR goals or your goals?

Are you helping others improve their lives?

Are you doing things that insure a thriving company or community?

This week, remember you are not truly a great leader unless you are helping others identify and achieve their successes.

Think . . . and act . . . like a leader!

"That whenever any Form of Government becomes destructive of these ends, it is the Right of the People to alter or to abolish it, and to institute new Government, laying its foundation on such principles and organizing its powers in such form, as to them shall seem most likely to effect their Safety and Happiness."

U.S. Declaration of Independence

Many leaders pride themselves on being independent. Many leaders think of the organizations they lead like their personal kingdoms. Many leaders let pride guide them and they abuse their power. Too many leaders ignore all the warning signs subordinates or followers give them. In other words, many leaders make the same mistakes the King of Great Britain made in the 18th century.

Usually when we read the Declaration of Independence we focus on the truths "we hold self-evident" and what every man should feel entitled to. We hardly ever list, talk about, or consider the specific complaints the colonists detailed about the leader they were revolting against.

But when I recently reviewed the Declaration of Independence I was struck by how similar many of the complaints our forefathers had against the King of Great Britain were to complaints people have in the workplace (and in volunteer leadership roles in associations) today.

This week, re-read the Declaration of Independence and pay attention to the list of grievances against the King that were included in the original document. Then ask yourself, "Could people be saying these things about me and my leadership style?"

Think . . . and act . . . like a leader!

"In order to have a conversation with someone you must reveal yourself."
James Baldwin

Have you ever worked with someone for more than a year then realized you really don't know anything about them? They never let you in on their thought process. They talk to lots of people but generally they are giving orders not engaging others in brainstorming, dialogue or problem-solving. They position every decision based on external factors. Or, worse, they frequently speak with passion but their actions don't match up to the message they say is so personally driven.

If you have met, or worked with, somebody like this they probably think they are a great leader because they talk to lots of people. And they think they give great speeches that, in their opinion, motivate others toward excellence.

But this Baldwin quote reminds us that people see straight through our phony facades.

We are the ones who are crazy when we believe we have fooled people into believing we care about them (or the work we are asking them to do) but never let them in to know us, understand us and truly interact with us.

It is true that as a leader you can't have a close personal relationship with every individual in your department, team or organization. But the pattern you establish with those you work with most closely will permeate the entire organization.

What is YOUR reputation? Do you have real conversations . . . or just one way monologues?

Think . . . and act . . . like a leader!

"Whenever you hear someone's name, take a moment to sense something of the greatness behind it."

Robert K Cooper

This quote is in Cooper's book, "The Other 90%: How to Unlock Your Vast Untapped Potential for Leadership and Life."

I have read this book at least 5 times since it was published in 2001. Each time, depending on what's going on in my life, different elements stand out. But every time I've read it I've been reminded that it really is the little things we do, or don't do, that make the biggest difference.

It doesn't always matter how smart you are if you are smart about how you treat people. And this particular quote made me stop and think about the importance of names.

A person's name doesn't only represent him or her. That name represents parents, marriages, grandparents and previous generations.

The names we walk around with today connect us to centuries of love and struggle, dreams and disasters.

When I meet someone new I try to not only listen to the name in order to remember it; I also try to take in the possible history that is attached to the name. I try to imagine that I am meeting not only this person but his or her ancestors.

Try it! See if it doesn't make you immediately more respectful and more curious about the person.

Think . . . and act . . . like a leader!

"Just a few words on time management: Forget all about it"

Tim Ferriss

Actually Tim goes on to say, "In the strictest sense, you shouldn't be trying to do more in each day, trying to fill every second with a work fidget of some type . . . Being busy is most often used as a guise for avoiding the few critically important but uncomfortable actions."

I know I'm not the only one who sometimes thinks, "How could I have accomplished so little when I've been so busy the last 8 hours, 8 days or 8 weeks?" It's times like that when I regroup and reprioritize.

The key to getting the right things done is having the right priorities and letting those priorities guide your choices. It means you have to stop doing things out of habit. It means you change who you take calls from, who you allow to interrupt you and how you delegate.

There are probably dozens of tasks I could do but only a few I must do.

This week, take a look at your priorities and see if that doesn't help you manage your time better (by only doing the most critical tasks and eliminating as much of the other stuff as possible).

And, if you need tips check out the book the quote came from: "The 4-Hour Workweek."

Think . . . and act . . . like a leader!

"If you can articulate a vision that makes people passionate, there are so many amazing things you can do."

Sophie Vandebroek

Sophie Vandebroek received the National Medal of Technology for her role in driving innovation for Xerox. Her job title is "Inventor-in-Chief" and it is her job to identify innovations that will become a competitive edge for her company.

What would happen if every leader took responsibility for driving innovation? I don't mean innovation just for the sake of change or trying something new. I mean innovation that is strategic, life-changing, brings in or serves customers in new ways and makes more money.

Most managers have their head buried in the tasks of today. Or, if they are future focused they are building plans for the future based on today's tools, resources and technologies.

Can you imagine what your organization would be like if all leaders - including you - felt it was their responsibility to be innovative? Would that make your organization more competitive, more successful or more amazing?

I bet it would. This week, pretend you are being coached by Sophie and practice articulating your vision in a way that makes people passionate. And if you can't do that, maybe you need a new vision!

(But we'll save that for a future issue of LeaderThink®)

Think . . . and act . . . like a leader!

"Supporting others in the organization to take a leadership role is healthy and in no way diminishes or threatens your own leadership role."

Mim Carlson / Margaret Donohoe

Are you a leader who wants all the attention on you? Are you threatened by someone else who is strong?

My theory about leadership is that the more people I can help to perform at their best, the easier my job will be!

If I can help another person do excellent work, make a contribution to the organization and maybe even get promoted then that's one more ally I have who will support me as I try to succeed.

If there are peers, who you can encourage to go for their next big success you should do so. They will always remember that you were one of their cheerleaders. They will usually look for ways to return the favor. And you help the organization achieve its goals.

If there are subordinates you can support as they build their skills don't hesitate to do so. You shouldn't be afraid they will surpass you. While they are reporting to you they will do more work and gain greater visibility for your team. If they promote out of your department, or move on to another organization, they will remember you were "in their corner" and gave them the direction, support and mentoring they needed to grow.

Great leaders partially evaluate their success based on how many other great leaders they create.

Think . . . and act . . . like a leader!

"Self-starters have discovered the value of initiative, but self-starters at some point must encourage others to assume responsibility, discover their own solutions, take action, and initiate follow-through on their own."

Len Ellis

You're a self-starter. You get things done. People know they can count on you to do what you say you do and more. You are GREAT as an individual contributor.

But as a leader, it is not possible for you to succeed long-term if you don't nurture others to take responsibility and get things done without your direct supervision.

How you delegate tasks and responsibilities can make a huge difference. If you assign tasks to others but make them come to you for approval or direction at every stage that only serves to restrain initiative in others. They will not risk going too far away from the explicit boundaries you set since it seems you want it done exactly the way you would do it. There is no reward for coming up with a personal, unique or different approach.

If you, on the other hand, delegate tasks and responsibilities but give no direction and leave someone to "sink or swim" you also may have more problems than successes. Developing initiative is not about working alone; in fact it often requires extraordinary skills for marshalling the talents and resources of others to accomplish a goal. So don't use the "assign and then abandon" approach either.

Find a balance.

This week recognize when others are demonstrating initiative and thank them for it.

Think . . . and act . . . like a leader!

"The closer one gets to the top, the more one finds there is no top"

Nancy Barcus

Have you been climbing the corporate ladder taking one rung at a time to get to the top? Are you the Board member who has stepped on others in order to get to what you thought was the "power" position you desired?

Go talk to others who have achieved positions of power and jobs with great responsibility. They will tell you that they still have others to report to or stakeholders who they are accountable to.

The successful and happy ones will also tell you that they are still on a journey to achieve their goals - that even in their current role of power or privilege they have new goals they are positioning themselves to achieve.

Great leaders know that true growth never ends. Titles don't define the person. And the top is just a plateau or landing that provides a brief resting place before you start the next set of stairs.

Think . . . and act . . . like a leader!

"Do not be afraid to set high goals because when you get there you will still have more to achieve."
Tracy Brown

About 20 years ago I reported to an executive who told me, "Take your time; you don't have to achieve all these goals in one year. What will you do next year?"

I listened to him and thought, "Well, once I check off half of these things I'll know what needs to be done next year." But per his request I whittled my official goals list in half. I still accomplished everything that was on the original list because in my mind, those were the priority things that needed to get done to set us up for long-term success.

I was not afraid that there would be nothing left to do if I achieved the original list of goals. Great leaders know that success is not a singular, clearly defined destination; it's all about making progress. And each step of progress allows you to see the next level of progress you can implement. It is a never-ending journey that true leaders love.

Think . . . and act . . . like a leader!

"Fail with enthusiasm"
Mary Anne Radmacher

Mary Anne Radmacher's book, "Lean Forward into Your Life (Begin Each Day as if it were On Purpose)" is not a traditional book on leadership. In fact, it's not a leadership book at all.

But in her creative nudging to choose how you want to live your life there are dozens of leadership lessons.

"Fail with enthusiasm" does not mean, to me, to plan to fail. But instead it reminds me that if I allow fear of failure to lead I will not take the risks I need to take to achieve extraordinary results.

And, when after my best efforts, I recognize I am going down the wrong track . . . I can accept failure not as a mistake but as a learning opportunity. Then I can enthusiastically evaluate my options and choose a new approach or my next steps.

Great leaders know that every effort will not produce excellence, success or perfection.

There will be failures along the way: things that didn't go quite the way you planned or hoped.

When that happens you have a choice. Choose to go into the next risk with enthusiasm instead of fear.

Think . . . and act . . . like a leader!

"Courage is the atom of change."

Bettina R Flores

Are you a change agent or a change avoider?

If I interviewed people who work with you what would they tell me about your courage in times of change?

When things are not working or are not going well it's easy to change. You want to rid yourself of the pain so you bravely try something new. But it still requires courage to try the "right" things instead of simply changing for the sake of change.

Embracing change when things are not broken, or are just difficult but not hopeless, requires both vision and courage.

Great leaders find the courage to guide individuals and organizations into new territory. Great leaders know that the only path to progress requires change . . . and change requires courage.

Think . . . and act . . . like a leader!

"No matter how far a person can go, the horizon is still way beyond you."
Zora Neale Hurston

Ambition. It is good to have ambition. But do not fool yourself into thinking (or believing) that your achievements are so extraordinary that you are the only one who can do what you are doing.

Great leaders use their ambition to improve the organization they are leading in ways that set up the next leadership team for even greater success.

Think . . . and act . . . like a leader!

"Place your hand over your chest and feel your heartbeat. That is actually your life clock ticking, counting down the moments you have left. One day it will stop. That is 100 percent guaranteed, and there's absolutely nothing you can do about it."
Bradley Trevor Greive

Being a leader is hard work. Being a leader is a big responsibility.

Being a leader is important. But being a leader isn't everything.

Great leaders understand that leadership is only part of their life. Leadership - at work, at home, in the community - is only worth it if you are intentional about two things.

First, be a leader who makes a positive difference in the lives and success of others.

Second, be a leader who understands his or her leadership style and decisions as a leader are creating a living and lasting legacy.

If leadership, for you, is primarily about control, prestige and superiority you might become a powerful person but you'll never be a great leader.

Think . . . and act . . . like a leader!

"Do not wait for ideal circumstances nor the best opportunities; they will never come."
Janet Erskine Stuart

I have a close friend who has great ideas and unlimited potential. He's smart. He is talented. And he has a mind for business that borders on pure genius.

But one of his few weaknesses is that he waits for the perfect circumstance and the ideal environment to make a commitment.

As a result, he hasn't achieved that much in terms of tangible results.

Everyone who talks to him about a deal, or an investment or some other idea he has for building a business gives him rave reviews. People get excited. Others want to get on board and get started building toward his vision. But he blocks the progress or slows the momentum because the circumstances are not ideal.

Perfection doesn't appear. The elements that can result in a perfect solution may all be present but they require some molding, tweaking or reconfiguring in order to show up as the needed answer to the question at hand.

Be a leader who takes people to success using whatever is available today to build a foundation that supports the success you are striving for tomorrow.

Think . . . and act . . . like a leader!

"A good goal is like strenuous exercise. It makes you stretch."
Mary Kay Ash

If you have attended a seminar on goal-setting it is very likely that you have been exposed to SMART goals. The acronym SMART represents goals that are Specific, Measurable, Attainable, Realistic and Timed. (Or some slight variation on these five words)

Sometimes when people are writing SMART goals they don't challenge themselves because they say, "In order for it to be attainable and realistic I need to be able to assure the outcome."

But I think Mary Kay Ash had the right idea. It's not really a goal if it doesn't require you to stretch. If it's not beyond your current capability then it is just a task on your to-do list. It's an action item. But it's not a goal.

Great leaders set solid goals for their own growth and development, as well as for the growth and development of their team members.

Think . . . and act . . . like a leader!

"Never tell people how to do things. Tell them what to do and they will surprise you with their ingenuity."
George S. Patton

Too many leaders think their job is to give people step by step instructions of the best way to do each task. Then they are confused when they get feedback that they come across as condescending, micro-managing or controlling.

Be very clear about the expected outcomes or deliverable. Be sure to explain deadlines and timetables. And assure your team that you are available to discuss ideas or suggestions. Then get out of the way!

Great leaders know their way of completing an assignment will likely work but it isn't the only way to accomplish the goal. Be available to provide feedback or even coaching if someone gets stuck. But don't dictate every aspect of project completion; and don't hover over every step of progress.

Think . . . and act . . . like a leader!

"Take risks. You can't fall off the bottom."
Barbara Proctor

Worried about making a mistake? Worried about doing something the wrong way? So worried about screwing it up that you don't ever start?

Get over yourself and take one step forward!

Now, I'm not advocating reckless action. I'm just nudging you to reach out and get some input from others. Or break your project into incremental steps you can achieve to build toward your success.

With sound analysis and a structured plan in place you can afford to take a few risks to achieve your goals.

And, as a leader, your team needs you to be willing to guide them through the unknown - and that is all a risk is. It's a situation where you step out on the faith that based on your best information and insight you have a chance to make progress or improve a relationship.

Great leaders take risks knowing that even if they don't achieve the intended result they will have learned more about what works - and what doesn't work. And that information will help guide the next steps that will lead to success!

Think . . . and act . . . like a leader!

"It is easy to be popular. It is not easy to be just."
Rose Elizabeth Bird

David had a reputation in the company of being a really nice guy. He was friendly, funny and talked to everyone with ease. David was popular.

David also had a reputation of being a terrible manager. People said he showed favoritism to the people he liked the most and sometimes when he thought he was joking around he made statements that were sexist. His subordinates didn't trust him to make fair decisions in employee relations situations so they bypassed him and went directly to the Human Resources department. Or they didn't say anything at all and just started looking for a new job.

People liked David as a person but they didn't respect him as a leader. Are you perceived by others to be like David?

Great leaders would choose being just over being popular (although most great leaders are perceived by others as both just and popular).

Think . . . and act . . . like a leader!

"What would you be doing if you knew you only had 37 days to live?"
Patti Digh

It's really quite simple. Are you doing things that are important to you? Are you honoring people who are important to you? And at work . . . are you leading in a way that leaves the legacy you want to survive you?

Patti Digh's blog "37 Days" is one of the places I go when I need to shift my priorities, remember my mission and simply be inspired to make good choices. (http://www.37days.typepad.com/37days/)

If you learned today that you only had 37 days remaining in your life, would you change the way you interact with others? If your answer is yes, then make those changes now.

Think . . . and act . . . like a leader!

"Gettin' good players is easy. Gettin' 'em to play together is the hard part."
Casey Stengel

How proud are you of the key players on your team? You have great people working with you, you know. But does your leadership style encourage them to work together as a team, or to compete with each other for your attention and favor?

One of my clients is a very smart guy but a terrible leader. Let's call him Jake.

Jake inherited a team in which half the members were really strong contributors and half were inconsistent in achieving tangible outcomes. Jake's strategy was to ignore the lower achievers, withhold information from them and hope they would resign or leave.

He spent time one-on-one with each of the team members he considered high-achievers and gave them lots of praise. But he rarely shared a team vision and he never allowed team members to work together to achieve a goal.

In fact, he fed different (and often conflicting) information to different team members which prevented them from collaborating on projects or supporting each other's efforts.

Before long, this team began to implode. I was called in by Jake's boss to design and facilitate a 6-month team building strategy after a few resignations. And others who relied on the team for information, guidance and support were complaining that Jake was the only one who had the information they needed and that he didn't trust others on the team to make any decisions or provide any services without his personal approval.

Some people thought Jake was a control freak. Others thought he was insecure and in over his head. But Jake was just a guy who had been promoted every 2-3 years because he was good at managing ideas, and great at managing himself. It wasn't totally his fault that he was not very effective accomplishing results through other people; his previous bosses had never held him accountable for developing and leveraging relationships.

Jake had to learn the difference between managing and leading. It wasn't easy for him to guide, coach and trust others; but he is learning how to do it. And along the way he was surprised to discover that some of the people he considered weak members of the team turned out to be star players once they had the information and encouragement they needed to do a great job!

Great leaders inspire each individual to perform at a high level while generating team effort as well.

Think . . . and act . . . like a leader!

"It is easy to fall back on recipes and forget what is in the pantry."
Leipper Management Group

Take a few ingredients, mix them together in a specific way and you have a great meal, right? And if that recipe works well for you, every time you need to entertain guests, or prepare something for a potluck dinner, you pull out that recipe because you know it works.

You may have other ingredients in the pantry but you don't want to try a new combination because you're not sure how the meal will turn out.

You might see a new product in the grocery store, but you don't buy it because you're not quite sure how to use it or how it might change your proven recipe.

Is any of this sounding familiar?

So is this how you lead others? Take a few people you know well, mix them together in ways you are very familiar with from past successes, and you have a great team.

When you have a high-profile assignment do you go to the same few people all the time because you know you can count on them and aren't so sure about some of the other people on your team?

And when new people come to the team you just substitute them for the missing ingredient and expect them to add the exact same flavor as the previous team member, right?

Wrong.

If this is how you lead others you are not leading at all. You are simply trying to recreate what has worked for you in the past with completely different people.

Great leaders know that each person is a unique ingredient in the recipe for workplace success.

Think . . . and act . . . like a leader!

"People ask the difference between a leader and a boss . . . the leader works in the open, and the boss in covert. The leader leads, and the boss drives."
Theodore Roosevelt

If you have a title, give orders and tell people what they need to do and how you want them to do it you are probably more a boss than a leader.

Often some of the strongest leaders don't have the most powerful titles, but people line up to receive their guidance, feedback and suggestions for success.

Every organization needs both bosses and leaders . . . but the best work environment is created when the person who is boss by title is also a great leader.

Think . . . and act . . . like a leader!

"We're more organized but less spontaneous, less alive. We're better prepared for the future but less able to enjoy the present. We're always going somewhere, never being anywhere. Just where are we going anyway? Where is there?"

Richard Leider & David Shapiro

Always going somewhere. Never being anywhere. Does this describe you?

How can you be an effective leader if you don't revel in the successes and challenges right before you today?

How can you truly connect with your team members if you are always planning for tomorrow and never engaged with who they are right now?

Great leaders spend time being organized and planning for tomorrow. But they also spend time recognizing and enjoying the experience of this day.

Think . . . and act . . . like a leader!

"The measure of success is not whether you have a tough problem to deal with, but whether it's the same problem you had last year."

John Foster Dulles

Think back 12 months. What were the biggest problems you were facing then?

Now fast-forward to today. Are you facing the same problems?

Great leaders do a consistent job of resolving problems and issues before moving on to new challenges.

I once worked with a manager who thought he was a good leader. He was a good "front man" for his organization; he spoke well and carried himself professionally. When problems were discussed he made it seem as if everything was under control.

But those of us who worked with him behind the scenes knew two things. First, we knew if a problem was particularly difficult he would simple remove it from the list of priorities so he wouldn't have to talk about it. His alternate method was to assign it to someone else to resolve.

Some of you are saying, "That's good delegation." But his assigning it to someone else wasn't about delegation; it was about avoidance. There is a big difference.

He would assign it to someone then act as if that problem (and often that person) didn't exist. He would not be available to troubleshoot or brainstorm solutions. He would not put the problem on the agenda to get input from others. He would simply act as if the problem didn't exist as long as he could.

Sometimes, the person he would assign one of these difficult problems to would actually resolve it; but never as a result of any guidance or input from him. More often, the person with the assignment would work diligently on symptoms related to the problem and make some progress. But as often as not, the root cause of the problem didn't get resolved and so the issue would escalate over time.

As a result, year after year there were 2-3 nagging problems that never went away. People outside of the department thought he was an up and coming leader because of his surface appearance. But when the problems got to the point where they could no longer be swept under the rug, this manager lost the respect of his peers, lost his reputation AND lost his job.

Great leaders get to the root cause of problems and create systems to resolve them. They coach others to respond to similar problems in the future and they insure there are fail-safes in place to prevent recurrences of the same problem. Then they move on to the next challenge.

Think . . . and act . . . like a leader!

"There are some words that close a conversation like an iron door."

Alexandre Dumas

"We've tried that before."
"We don't do it that way around here"
"That's a stupid idea."
"When I want your opinion I'll ask for it."

This week, listen to the conversation at your meetings; and especially monitor what YOU say. How often do the words you use cut someone down? How many times each week do you send the message to others that their ideas are unwelcome? Just how much do you encourage; and how much do you discourage the people you work with?

As leaders, our words really do matter. We can use them to build others up. Or we can use them to cut people down.

Great leaders have a reputation for positive communication. They regularly use words to encourage the team to participate. They use words that establish an inclusive environment. They model the communication style their team members can use with each other and with customers.

Instead of ending conversations and discouraging discussion, great leaders set the tone for maximum engagement.

Think . . . and act . . . like a leader!

"You can reposition yourself regardless of your age, regardless of your circumstance."

T.D. Jakes

In his book "Reposition Yourself: Living a Life without Limits" Bishop T.D. Jakes instructs the reader to ask himself the question, "Am I really living life to the fullest?"

Sometimes we are not the best leaders we can be because we would rather be doing something else. Does that describe you?

Would you really rather be working in a different organization or on a different project?

Would you actually prefer to be on a different career path?

Did you love your job five years ago but now it's simply boring and repetitive?

If your answer to these or other similar questions is yes, then it is almost impossible for you to be a great leader in your current situation.

Take Jakes' advice and reposition yourself. Consider where your talents and passion can best be used and start moving in that direction.

Great leaders have passion that shows because they love what they are doing.

Think . . . and act . . . like a leader!

"If you are on a beach and a tsunami hits, you'll drown whether you're a small child or an Olympic swimmer."

Lloyd Blankfein (CEO of Goldman Sachs)

No matter how good you are you are not invincible. When interviewed by Fortune Magazine (following a year where his company had achieved its highest profits ever) Mr. Blankfein said it was important to stay prepared for changing conditions.

As a leader, it can be tempting to believe our vision and skills have led to great success and that success will continue because, well, we are such a great leader. But in reality, the unexpected ups and downs are the biggest challenges.

The market conditions we couldn't anticipate catch us off guard. The human error someone in our organization is responsible for can create a major public relations disaster. Members or customers have a bad experience and stop trusting us. These things can happen and are out of the control of the leader.

Great leaders celebrate their successes but never fail to prepare for unexpected challenges, for that is when their talent and skill will be most tested.

Think . . . and act . . . like a leader!

"The true test of character is not how much we know how to do, but how we behave when we don't know what to do."

Jon Holt

It is so easy to look good and to be successful when you are doing something you have done before. You know the pitfalls and you avoid them. You know what doesn't work, so you focus on process steps that will lead you and your team to success.

Your leadership skills are not the key to success in a situation like this. You are simply repeating what's worked in the past. You are just going through the motions.

How you lead when the situation is new, when the entire team is different, or when an emergency you never expected occurs . . . those are the times when your leadership ability is really put to the test.

Are you ready to step into leadership in unpredictable circumstances? Are you confident about your ability to assess the situation and use the right combination of skills and talents to get the job done? More importantly, are the people who need to follow you confident you can lead in unpredictable times? Do they trust and respect you?

If you work in an environment where you can make a plan and everything pretty much follows that plan then don't worry about this. But if you, like most of us, know that something happens every month (or every week or every day) that you could not have predicted and people depend on you to set the tone; then you need to be concerned.

Great leaders are skilled at dealing with the unexpected. They practice asking the right kind of questions. They know the talent of their team and are able to reconfigure work assignments to accomplish new goals. When things are going smoothly they build the kind of relationships that will engender trust and support when emergencies occur or when changes in direction are needed.

Think . . . and act . . . like a leader!

"We will be known forever by the tracks we leave."
American Indian (Dakota) Proverb

As a leader, what tracks are you leaving?

Think . . . and act . . . like a leader!

"Now I'm done believing you. You don't know what I'm feeling. I'm more than what you made of me. I followed the voice you think you gave to me. But now I gotta find my own"

Deena Jones

In the song "Listen" Deena Jones (in the film Dreamgirls) makes a powerful attempt to let her husband / manager know his failure to take her dreams, needs and desires into consideration is making her consider leaving.

Of course, you are not "married" to the people you work with, but how many of them would say your biggest priority seems to be to remake them into YOUR image of who they should want to be? Are you so busy pushing them into your vision of who they are, how they should behave and what they should care about that you have no idea of their own desires, their own perceptions about their talents and potential?

Great leaders find a way to tap into each individual's talents and dreams while also inspiring them to work toward mutually beneficial goals.

Think . . . and act . . . like a leader!

"It was the people who moved their leaders, not the leaders who moved the people . . . A leader who understands this kind of mandate knows that he must be sensitive to the anger, the impatience, the frustration, the resolution that have been loosed in his people. Any leader who tries to bottle up these emotions is sure to be blown asunder in the ensuing explosion."

Martin Luther King, Jr.

Most people would agree that Martin Luther King Jr was a great leader. He had vision. He was a master strategist. He was one of the most eloquent and powerful speakers of the 20th century.

But in an essay he wrote in 1964 he made it clear that one of the major reasons he was effective was because he was simply taking people where THEY wanted to go.

There were times when he had to convince them the path he was recommending was going to lead to the destination they were determined to reach. But it was always their chosen destination.

What about you?

As a leader do you find yourself telling people what is the best destination for them, and spending lots of time trying to convince them? Do you find you are going in one direction while they are going in another?

If so, maybe you should do a better job of listening to where the people want to go and what they want to achieve. Or alternatively, you could focus on giving them information and soliciting their input in order to get them to agree that your vision for the future is one they can embrace as their own.

Great leaders know it is easier to lead a group moving with speed and passion toward a common goal.

Think . . . and act . . . like a leader!

"If you cannot find peace within yourself, you will never find it anywhere else."

Marvin Gaye

Do you find yourself constantly complaining about other people? Do you have a hard time trusting the people you work with most closely?

When things go wrong do you focus on finding a person to blame or a solution that will change the outcome?

Is the work you do a representation of your best or simply a way to pass the time and collect a paycheck?

Great leaders are able to make a difference because they are at peace with themselves. They have a vision and are passionate about the work they are doing. Their ego is under control. They have a certain peace that comes from clarity. They are able to focus on including others because they have accepted their own strengths and weaknesses.

Find your inner peace and help others do the same.

Think . . . and act . . . like a leader!

"There are two ways of exerting one's strengths: one is pushing down, the other is pulling up."

Booker T Washington

What kind of leader are you?

Do people think of you as pushing them down, keeping them in "their place", and always having things done your way? Do they see you as strong, but rigid?

Or, do people perceive you as a strong leader who is a great mentor, an advocate for others' success and a person who makes it easy for everyone around you to do their best?

It's your choice . . .

Think . . . and act . . . like a leader!

"Innovation is super fragile. It's very easy to kill. We need a stubborn, rebellious attitude."

Douglas Merrill

Stop. Think. Remember that coworker you described as difficult, nonconformist, or just plain crazy?

Maybe that was the most innovative person you've ever met but you couldn't recognize the value they offered because they didn't approach work the same way you did.

As a leader it's hard to nurture creativity and maintain order at the same time. But successful leaders find ways to encourage innovation.

And sometimes, taking your team or your organization to the next level REQUIRES new responses to old problems.

Consider the people you currently lead.

If I interviewed them would they tell me you allow them to turn a problem inside out and find a new solution?

Or would they say you're a nice person but you want nice, clean solutions that match your understanding of every situation?

Get out of your team's way.

Read the March 2008 issue of Fast Company Magazine and learn why GOOGLE is number one. Plus learn what leaders like Douglas Merrill do to earn a spot in the "World's 50 Most Innovative Companies" list.

Think . . . and act . . . like a leader!

"Frequent effective communication builds trust, which, in turn, leads to more open and meaningful communication."

Richard D. Bucher

I can remember working with a supervisor who communicated every hour throughout every day with his staff. But almost everything he said, or sent by email, included a criticism, a tone of disrespect or an accusation.

Frequent communication alone does not necessarily build trust.

A different leader I once reported to was very effective when communicating with her direct reports. She shared both good news and bad news. She provided both praise and constructive criticism in an appropriate way. But we had to track her down to get any of that information.

So effective - but episodic – communication doesn't always build trust either if people are unsure if they are receiving the information they need to do their jobs well.

Great leaders consider both content and timing when deciding what, when and how to communicate with different stakeholders.

Think . . . and act . . . like a leader!

"Leadership and domination are NOT synonyms."
Tracy Brown

Effective leaders have great power. They are influential; they are trend setters. They are people others follow. But the people who follow, support and admire great leaders are followers by choice.

Both domination and leadership require clear vision and personal strength. Both require you to make difficult decisions, sometimes with limited information. And both result in a group of people doing what you have pronounced as important and valuable.

But the two approaches to getting things done are very different.

Despite what some people in powerful positions believe, you are not a leader simply because you have power over others. Some people might follow your orders because they are paid to do so. Others might go along with your ideas because they don't want to make waves. And many will do what you say because they are afraid to question or challenge you. But don't confuse your domination over them for leadership.

Domination gets you results the way you want them for the reason you want them. Leadership achieves results everyone is proud of and invested in.

Domination puts you in charge or your own little kingdom. Leadership puts you in charge of creating an environment that honors and provides for others.

Great leaders are strong and use their power to include and serve others.

Think . . . and act . . . like a leader!

"A drum major with no band is just a fool dancing on a football field!"

Dalton Sherman

Picture a drum major . . . waving arms, announcing the next moves, directing the band from one formation to the next . . . and doing so with dramatic gestures, a commanding voice and an entertaining flourish that captures the on-looking crowd.

If there was no band following this drum major's instructions and movements he or she would definitely look a little strange.

Are you a leader without a following?

Are you barking orders, making a big scene and doing things you think make you look good . . . but when you turn around you find few, if any, people inspired and engaged by your efforts?

Nine-year old Dalton Sherman is the 2008 winner of the Martin Luther King Jr. Oratory Contest sponsored by the law firm Gardere Wynne Sewell. The quote above was the closing line of his winning speech. He might be "just a kid" but his wisdom applies to us all.

Don't be a person who is just "actin' a fool" and deluding yourself into believing you're leading. Some of the greatest drum majors, like great leaders, understand that talent and visibility help, but building trust, earning respect and practicing effective communication are critical to success.

Think . . . and act . . . like a leader!

"A great leader's courage to fulfill his vision comes from passion, not position."

John Maxwell

Are you passionate about the work you are doing?

Are you passionate about the people you work with and the people you serve?

Or, are you just doing what your job requires you to do . . . or what your boss expects you to complete?

You can be a very effective (project) manager without passion. If you have competence or commitment you can get things done. But to be a great leader working on a great vision, you have to have passion about the vision you are trying to make happen.

It is that passion that attracts followers.

It is that passion that sustains your energy when the odds are against you.

It is passion that helps you create innovative solutions to unforeseen problems.

When added to communication skills and interpersonal relationship-building skills, passion is the great leader's secret weapon.

Think . . . and act . . . like a leader!

"When I hire somebody, they have to be really smart. But the real issue for me is: are they going to fall in love with Apple? If they do, everything else will take care of itself."

Steve Jobs

When you have the opportunity to hire a new employee or recruit a new member to your nonprofit Board or a work-related project team, do you define the best candidate as the one who is the smartest? Or the one who has the most experience? Or the 'best' education?

What about the candidate who cares the most about your organization, project or mission?

I have heard hiring managers eliminate some outstanding candidates from consideration because the candidates were TOO passionate about the project or organization. They have said, "Well, Person-A really gets what we are about, but Person-B has an MBA from Harvard." Then they choose the prestige of the Ivy League education over the person who clearly is aligned with the organization's mission and values.

On the other hand, it would not be smart to hire someone who only has passion. Obviously each person you bring on to your team should have applicable education and experience they can apply to help your organization achieve its goals.

I have experienced far too many disasters when people were selected because of their passion and excitement but they clearly did not have the leadership or communication skills required to be effective in their assigned roles. Their performance (or lack thereof) led the entire team, and their organizations, into a slow death spiral resulting in mistrust, frustration, anger, decreased revenue, and high levels of turnover.

As Steve Jobs, CEO and co-founder of Apple reminds us, we need to surround ourselves with people who have both. It is important to hire smart people but it is just as important to select people who love what our organization is about so much that they will find ways to make us better.

Think . . . and act . . . like a leader!

"The role of the leader is changing. The new role is to help people face reality and to mobilize them to make change."
Ronald Heifetz

More than 10 years ago, Harvard University professor Ronald Heifetz chronicled the changes facing managers who wanted to be effective. In the 21st century the difference between managers and leaders has continued to evolve.

What about in your organization? Who are the best -- and the most respected -- leaders?

In most organizations the people who would be recognized for their leadership skills are not necessarily the people with the most powerful titles.

In fact, often the people with the biggest titles are considered the worst leaders because they insulate themselves from the real people working on the real issues. Or they are avoided because they are condescending and make decisions based on their personal preferences instead of taking into consideration the people who will be affected by their decisions.

The best leaders are able to mobilize people to get things done - not just because they send out an order for compliance, but because they are connected, respected and able to communicate.

What about you? Are you a 21st century leader . . . or are you stuck in 20th century management mode?

Think . . . and act . . . like a leader!

"Later is a very sneaky opponent . . . It's always convincing you that whatever needs to be done will somehow be improved by waiting."

Sarano Kelley

I was talking with a fried last week who said, "I have so much to do I have to prioritize. Some things just have to wait for later."

I could really relate to that. There always seems to be so much going on. All of us must decide which items to check off our "to do" list today and which items to push into tomorrow, next week, next month or next year.

If we are good leaders we also choose which items on our list can be delegated or transferred to others.

So my question for you is this: Are you a prioritizer . . . or just a procrastinator? There really is a difference.

The phrase, "I'll do it later" or "I'll get to that tomorrow" comes up a lot, as if just by saying it we create more time to do more things at some unknown future time. But we each have only a few hours each day to be productive. Later can be a sedative that lulls us into the fantasy that we can do more than we actually can - or should.

During the coming week, monitor how often you think or say, "I'll do it later." Each time ask yourself, "Is this something I should be doing or should I be passing it on to someone else?"

If it's something you should delegate, pass it on.

If it's something you must do, then ask yourself, "Since I need to do this, why is it important and when does it need to be done?"

Then plan your schedule to allow you to complete the task when it is most important to do it. That might mean you rearrange your schedule to do it today or it might be you set date two weeks from now and stick with it.

Leaders who are effective get the right things done, delegate the tasks they shouldn't be doing and use the word "later" in an intentional way.

Think . . . and act . . . like a leader!

"There is a difference between being busy and being in a hurry."

Valorie Burton

Most of us have a long list of things we want to get done. We are busy all the time and we think that's good.

But regardless of how busy you are, is your preferred pace a fast or slow one? And what do you think about people whose pace is different from yours? Speed is not necessarily an indicator of a person's commitment or capability.

When you find yourself judging others because they speak or work
faster -- or slower -- than you prefer, shift your thinking to whether or not they get the job done in a quality way within the mutually agreed upon deadlines.

Then, ask yourself, "Is my pace helping me - or hurting me – in getting my work done and in building relationships with others?"

Do you think by going faster you'll get more done and be more successful? Has going faster every resulted in you skipping an important detail or missing your quality goal? Speed is not always better!

Do you think by going slower you are more likely to achieve perfection? Have you missed critical deadlines or suffered paralysis from over-analysis? Going slower is not always the answer!

Adjusting your pace to insure a high quality result is the smart thing to do. And acknowledging the fact that the people you work with have different paces which are natural for them is an important way to support the success of your team.

Great leaders recognize the need to speed up and the need to slow down differs depending on the project, the person, the deadline and the type of work being done at the time.

Think . . . and act . . . like a leader!

"A good leader inspires others with confidence in him; a great leader inspires them with confidence in themselves."

Unknown Author

Be honest.

As a leader is your priority getting people to trust you or to trust themselves?

It is absolutely important that others trust you. They need to know you have the skills and the integrity to take your team or organization forward.

But it is just as important that you instill self-confidence in those on your team. If they know you trust them to do a great job and to take care of issues that arise within their scope of responsibility they will go above and beyond the minimum requirements.

People who are self-confident will take more risks and will help you grow your organization.

People who are self-confident will respond in crisis situations when you are not around to make decisions.

This week think do one thing that builds the self-confidence of at least one person on your team.

Think . . . and act . . . like a leader!

"Vacation (noun). A period of time devoted to pleasure, rest, or relaxation"
American Heritage Dictionary

Every good leader needs a vacation.

Vacations from our regular tasks and responsibilities serve so many purposes. Vacations help us:

- Release
- Recharge
- Remember

RELEASE
When we take a vacation we are able to release the silently building tension and stress of our regular routine. Even when we love the work we are doing, it creates stress that we are so accustomed to we "take it in stride." Vacations allow us to relax and let go of whatever tension might be going unnoticed.

RECHARGE
Vacations allow us to recharge our physical and emotional batteries. When we shift to fun and relaxing activities we tap into a different energy center in our minds and bodies.

REMEMBER

Toward the end of a vacation most of us begin to remember why we are so committed to the work we are getting ready to return to. We remember what we are good at and how our skills and talents are best utilized. Vacations give us a little distance from our day-to-day routine and help us reflect on, and remember, our primary motivations.

TWO ADDITIONAL BENEFITS

You are not the only person your vacation helps. When you go on vacation it helps to remind people who work with you that they have the ability to get things done without your daily presence. You empower them to utilize their skills and talents in creative and effective ways.

And . . . if you are a great leader . . . your vacation allows people to miss you and to be reminded why they honor, respect and depend upon you throughout the year.

Think . . . and act . . . like a leader!

"There are some people that if they don't know, you can't tell them."

Louis Armstrong

OK. Every one of us knows as least two people who think they know everything (or that they know everybody worth knowing). And when that person reports to you, serves on your Board of Trustees, or works as a colleague it can be very challenging to lead them in a direction they don't agree with.

Human nature would be for you to try to convince this person that your approach is right or that the group's decision is better than their individual preference. But no matter what you say, and no matter how many logical arguments you present you can't open a closed mind.

If this difficult-to-work-with person simply disagrees, but is not doing anything that sabotages your efforts, let it go. You don't need 100% agreement from every person for every initiative or activity.

Notice your irritation and frustration with this person and manage it by also remembering the positive contributions she has made to other projects. Don't forget the special skills or connections she may contribute to the team. And consider if there are ways to redirect her focus to the special talents she brings to the group.

However, if this person is behaving inappropriately or doing things that are in direct opposition to the established direction, you must act. There are only a few times when your rank or position power must be activated and this is one of them. In a private setting let this person know his behavior is inappropriate and why.

Re-state the agreed-upon objectives or activities and clearly prohibit the inappropriate actions he has been demonstrating.

If this person is a peer, and you don't have a leadership role that has the authority to correct this person, approach them as a friend and colleague and offer some feedback. Let him know the negative effect his words or actions are having on the entire group.

Don't over-react to a "know it all" type of person. And don't let personality differences divide your team. But also know when to step in as a leader to create appropriate boundaries.

Think . . . and act . . . like a leader!

"The greatest obstacle to discovery is not ignorance - it is the illusion of knowledge."

Daniel J. Boorstin

When we think we know something we don't search for more information.

When we believe we are the best at something, we ignore or discount the contributions and achievements of others.

When we feel our answer or approach is the solution to a problem, we fail to tap into creative or innovative approaches available to us.

Discovery requires an open mind to learning what we don't already know. It challenges us to suspend our judgments of others and to activate a child-like sense of curiosity about different ideas, beliefs, approaches and answers.

Great leaders use discovery as a tool to understand others and to achieve greater results from themselves.

Think . . . and act . . . like a leader!

"If I had known my son was going to be president of Bolivia, I would have taught him to read and write."
Enrique Penaranda's mother

Is there a person on your team who you don't bother to invest in because you don't believe they have much to offer?

If you are in a corporate leadership role, what if that person becomes the CEO of your organization 16 years from now? If you are in a nonprofit volunteer leadership role, what if that person leaves your committee, builds alliances with others and winds up as President of the Board of Trustees five years from now?

It is so easy to focus on the people who strike us as super talented, extremely aggressive and highly motivated. But great leaders seek the spark of genius in each person and fan that spark into a flame.

Help each person on your team be at their best as often as possible. See them as the people who will be the leaders, executives and thought leaders of tomorrow.

Think . . . and act . . . like a leader!

"Many of life's failures are people who did not realize how close they were to success when they gave up."
Thomas Edison

We have to recognize that sometimes persistence is the only bridge that connects our outcomes to our goal. It is the bridge that planning and execution travel to get us from the idea stage to the end of the project.

A couple weeks ago I was in a store and saw a paperweight that had the words, "It's not a failure until you give up." I thought about how many times I felt I had failed and wondered how many of those instances might have turned out differently if I had held on just a little longer?

Now, don't get me wrong. I do believe there are times to stop. I believe there are times we commit to things that are beyond our capabilities and it is appropriate to give the task over to someone who can achieve the goal.

Still it is interesting to reflect on the reality that there are times we give up just a little too soon.

So during the coming week, consider where you need to be persistent.

Think about how far you have come and how close you might be to achieving key goals in your life. Then recommit to do whatever it takes to earn the success you so desire.

Think . . . and act . . . like a leader!

"Have no fear of perfection -- you'll never reach it."
Salvadore Dali

How would your life be different if you stopped trying to be perfect?

How much easier would your relationships with others become if you stopped expecting other people to be perfect?

Perfect means there is no room for error or options or creativity.

Perfect is the best, the ultimate; it is outcome or behavior no one else can achieve.

But in business, and in life, there are so many ways to achieve desired outcomes. There are so many cultural norms that affect our daily behavior.

I find it impossible to believe that striving for perfection in everything we do is healthy or necessary.

Instead, I look to define excellence and think about what steps I can take to approach that level of performance. Excellence, to me, means performance that achieves a high standard but it doesn't mean I (or the outcome) need to be perfect.

Perfection is not the goal great leaders chase because perfection leaves out the human element.

Think . . . and act . . . like a leader!

"Complaints, whether they come from employees or customers, are a routine part of business."

Miller, Wackman, Nunnally & Saline

When someone complains our first reaction is often to get defensive. We want to explain why they shouldn't be upset, angry or disappointed. Or we want to justify why we did whatever we did to again prove to them they should not be complaining.

But what if, next time someone complains, you instead said, "You are absolutely right," then continued, "Tell me more so I am sure I understand where you are coming from and what I can do better next time."

As leaders, we often confuse being successful with being right or with being the best.

In reality, the best leaders are the ones people bring problems and complaints to because they know this leader will engage the right people, ask the right questions and create a solution.

Rarely is the best leader the one with all the answers.

Most often the best leader is the one who welcomes complaints and sees them as opportunities to improve or grow.

Think . . . and act . . . like a leader!

"I meant what I said, and I said what I meant. An elephant's faithful, One hundred percent."

From Horton Hears a Who (Dr Seuss)

Do you consistently mean what you say, and say what you mean?

Would the people who work with you describe your actions as being in total alignment with the words you speak?

Or are you like one leader I know who tells people what he wants them to hear while planning a completely different course of action?

He thinks he is a great leader but people who work with him view him as deceitful and disrespectful.

He thinks he is smarter than everyone else. But people who work with him simply save their brilliance for other projects and other people because their experience with this leader has taught them he can only hear and appreciate his own ideas and approaches.

Great leaders seem to instinctively know their words and their actions must communicate the same message. They set a personal standard (and provide a personal example) of alignment between their words and actions.

Think . . . and act . . . like a leader!

"Every victim has a dream that somehow has been denied or thwarted."

David Emerald

Are you aggravated by people in your life who always put themselves in the role of *victim*?

It can be very irritating when you know someone has the intelligence and the skills to complete a task or take on a project, but they always have an excuse for not performing well.

I don't want to imply that you should let these folks off the hook and simply allow them to play the victim role over and over. I, instead, want to ask you to step into the role of coach and ask the kinds of questions that will let you (and often the person playing victim) WHY they are stuck in this place of weakness.

When someone is blaming others and using that as a reason for withholding their own talents it usually means they were terribly hurt in a past attempt to be powerful, independent or successful.

If you can find out what situation caused them to back away from their true skills or caused them to lose self-confidence you might be able to help them step into their own greatness.

Helping others achieve excellence is what great leaders do.

Think . . . and act . . . like a leader!

"When people become more self-accountable they stop projecting and laying blame."
Colin Tipping

Nothing I have done (or failed to do) is anyone else's fault.

What would your team or organization be like if everyone had that attitude?

What would it be like if you, and every other person, took full responsibility for what you did (or did not do) and never shifted the blame to someone else?

Great leaders are able to identify failures in the process, mistakes made along the way and the affect of poor communication on achieving the desired results. But great leaders always claim responsibility for their contribution to the failure . . . then focus on changes in process or policy that will generate a different result "next time."

Think . . . and act . . . like a leader!

"Practice is everything."

Periander

This week, think about all the lessons you've learned over time about leadership and ask yourself this question: "Am I applying what I already know?"

Great leaders deliver consistently on the basics.

Think . . . and act . . . like a leader!

"Many of the things you can count don't count. Many of the things you can't count really count."
Albert Einstein

Good project managers are careful to establish and track things that can be measured. They consistently demonstrate excellence in setting and meeting deadlines, creating checkpoints and evaluating performance based on the quantity of work completed within a tightly structured framework.

Good leaders balance their project management skills with their people management skills. And often, managing people goes beyond keeping track of things you can count.

You can't count feelings, although you can recognize them.

You can't count engagement, although you know when someone is committed and involved.

You can't count confidence, although you can observe the behavior that demonstrates it.

You can't count potential, although you can imagine a great future for the people around you.

You can't count trust, although every relationship reflects the level of trust shared between the people involved.

Great leaders usually have good project management skills but they become recognized as leaders because of their talent and skill for managing people.

When great leaders don't have good project management skills they make sure someone on their immediate team is able to take on the tasks related to project management while they focus their energy on managing the things you can't count.

Think . . . and act . . . like a leader!

"Standing in the middle of the road is very dangerous; you get knocked down by the traffic from both sides."

Margaret Thatcher

Are you a manager who tries to make everyone happy?

Do you constantly avoid taking sides or stating your position because you don't want to explain or defend your actions?

Are you most comfortable with those who always agree with you - or who, at least, don't disagree with you about anything you consider important or valuable?

Great leaders have clear vision, make visible commitments and engage others in achieving shared goals. Sometimes engaging others means understanding different perspectives, working through disagreements, and accepting that everyone might not like you.

If you are not skilled in choosing a path, explaining that path to others and traveling that path with conviction then you aren't ready to be a great leader.

If you are more comfortable taking your direction from others you can be a great supervisor.

If you are more comfortable keeping the balance between workers and managers . . . or between customers and staff . . . you might be able to become a good project manager.

But, if you want to be viewed as a leader you must be able to do more than follow directions or negotiate between people with different perspectives. Great leaders have a clear perspective and are able to rally others around that vision.

Think . . . and act . . . like a leader!

"Fall seven times; stand up eight."
Japanese Proverb

Leaders should be the ones who are out ahead of the crowd considering new options and trying new approaches. If your fear of falling (failure) is stronger than your desire to fly (succeed) you won't take many risks.

I'm a roller skater. It's not unusual for people who are just learning to skate to say, "Wow! You skate so well. I've never seen you fall." But I always respond, "Oh yes . . . I fall several times a year. Anybody who is a really good skater knows falls are inevitable so when it happens we just drop, roll, get up and keep skating."

A few weeks ago I had a really bad fall and I wasn't even taking a major risk. The person I was skating with slipped and I was caught in the domino effect. It was a reminder that sometimes falls just happen and catch you totally by surprise! Falls are not always a result of your own actions.

I fell with such force and at such an angle, that the axle on one of my skates broke. But I stood up. I put some ice on my ankle while waiting for the broken axle to be replaced. Then 30 minutes later I got back out there to skate some more.

That's when I realized this was more serious than the typical little slip. Instead of ice making everything all better, I was dealing with more serious consequences: a sprained ankle and a pulled muscle in my foot. So that was going to require a few more interventions. But 5 weeks later I was back on my skates executing basic moves and in another 5-8 weeks I'll be back at 100%.

The attitude that 'falls will happen' can be applied to all parts of life. Great leaders are confident they can recover from a fall whether it's a minor slip or a major drop.

Think . . . and act . . . like a leader!

"When power translates itself into tyranny, the principles of that power are bankrupt."
James Baldwin

You are a leader. You have power.

Power, when used in a healthy way, helps you influence outcomes, engage the right stakeholders and create solutions that are mutually beneficial.

Power, when used in an unhealthy way, might get results but leaves casualties in its wake.

If I were to interview the 10 people who during the last 6 months worked most closely with you would they tell me you share power, hoard power or abuse power?

During the next week, ask for feedback from at least 3 different people. Ask them if they think you use your power responsibly.

Encourage them to give you examples of both good and bad ways you handle the power that comes with your position or role in the organization.

Review what they tell you looking for patterns and identify one thing you want to change or improve upon.

Think . . . and act . . . like a leader!

"The talent alarm is buzzing . . . don't even think about snoozing."
Ron Kupferman

Are you the kind of person who hits the snooze button when your alarm goes off in the morning? All of us have done that on one occasion or another. We just did not want to get out of the warm, cozy bed and face the challenges of the day.

But as a leader, when facing the challenge of planning to keep all positions filled (on our team, in our business unit, or organization wide) we can't afford to hit the snooze button.

The changing demographics, the expectations of people from different generational groups, technology updates and the shifting economy are just four of the many factors that challenge us to not only fill our current openings but to also develop a strategy that will help us attract and retain the people we need 1, 3 and 5 years from now.

Back to the alarm. Have you ever pressed the snooze button two, three or more times but then, once you finally got up and out into the day, you realized it was sunny, you were blessed and it was a great day to be alive?

Well, having a strategic plan for staffing can help you attract, identify and groom the best talent for your organization. So disable your "snooze" button and get on with it!

Great leaders understand they are responsible for what happens now--and in the future. Their decisions today shape their organization's success tomorrow.

Think . . . and act . . . like a leader!

"When an employee is in a job that does not allow them to feature their strengths, they are not likely to be highly engaged."

Michael Woodward

Despite our best efforts we have people who are not well suited for the positions they hold.

Do you resign yourself to poor or mediocre performance from that person? Or instead do you find a better alternative?

One of your first steps should be identifying the strengths that person has.

Are there ways to apply those strengths within the current position? Can some duties be shifted to a different person in a similar role? How can you let this employee show, and build upon his or her strengths instead of always focusing on the weaknesses?

This doesn't mean you totally ignore the weaknesses.

Provide training where it is needed. Coach for success where it will be helpful. Just don't try to force fit someone into a role they truly are not suited for.

Great leaders protect their investments in people by insuring each person has authentic opportunities to share their best skills and talents on a daily basis.

Think . . . and act . . . like a leader!

"The more you prove that the limits people assume to be in place for you really don't exist, the more you can accomplish"

David Paterson

It happens all the time. People look at you and see who they think you are. People read your name, or hear your voice, and create a picture in their mind about you. Even people who have known you for a long time have trouble imagining you doing something new or different from their past experience of you.

Sometimes these assumptions and stereotypes others have of you can get in the way of your next success.

When people judge your capabilities based on your ethnicity, age, national origin, known disability or other factor it can be difficult to change their mind. But what's most important is this: Don't let their image of you limit your own beliefs about who you are and what you can accomplish!

In March 2008, David Paterson became the first blind governor of any state in the U.S. He is also the first African American governor of that state and has a long list of other "firsts" he can claim. But he didn't achieve all he has achieved in order to say he was the first. His extraordinary leadership has always been about being the best David Paterson he could be.

Great leaders have an internal compass that guides them beyond the limits other people assume for them.

Think . . and act . . . like a leader!

"One of the true tests of leadership is the ability to recognize a problem before it becomes an emergency."

Arnold H. Glasgow

It takes a certain kind of person to walk into an emergency situation and "save" the team, the organization or the community. There is a unique combination of management and leadership skills required to successfully turn a crisis into an opportunity.

But a great leader often avoids crisis by recognizing the trend, by listening to people and by engaging the right resources to understand the problem and craft a proactive response.

This is not to imply that leaders never face emergencies. There will always be acts of nature and business surprises that could not have been forecast. Strong leaders, however, will not let industry shifts, economic trends, expectations of employees or a changing target market population catch them off guard.

So, don't get complacent! Notice the changes and trends that affect your organization. And always ask yourself, "How might this create problems (or opportunities) for us?" Then use the resources you have to prepare for the future.

Think . . . and act . . . like a leader!

"The world is more malleable than you think and it's waiting for you to hammer it into shape."
Bono

Of course there are rules and policies and cultural norms. There are procedures that have existed for decades or longer. There are lots of people around to tell you how to do things, what works and what doesn't.

But sometimes, what you have known to work in the past is not the only way to get things done. Sometimes people are ready for change . . . and policies are no longer effective.

Great leaders learn to recognize when to tweak existing processes and when to ask people for new ideas.

Think . . . and act . . . like a leader!

Some Closing Thoughts

Leadership is challenging. But it can also be very rewarding.

If you are like me, you need reminders on a regular basis to step up to the leadership challenge. Sometimes it would be so much easier to pout or procrastinate. Some days you just don't want to be bothered with putting others first. And all of us have months where we are so busy we just feel overwhelmed.

My goal is to remind you that leadership is the result of your daily, weekly and monthly choices. My goal is to encourage you to make being the best leader you can be a priority.

And in reminding you I remind myself that there is no magic to being a leader. It just requires making a conscious choice to make a positive difference.

You are now a part of the LeaderThink® family. Let us all be examples of leaders who are trustworthy, caring, courageous and fair.

Tracy Brown

About Tracy Brown

Tracy grew up in St. Louis, Missouri and attended public schools there. At school and at church she was expected to be a leader and to make a positive difference in the world. As a result, Tracy has achieved high goals in her profession and in her community.

She has served as a volunteer leader for more than a dozen community-based organizations involved in health care, the performing arts and improving life for previously homeless or disadvantaged individuals. She is one of the creators of the Dallas Dinner Table process, which brings people together in small groups to increase understanding about the impact of race and racism in the daily lives of local citizens. And she actively volunteers with the Center for Nonprofit Management helping leaders in agencies nationwide improve their ability to lead.

Tracy is President of Diversity Trends, LLC, a consulting and training firm based in Dallas, Texas. She helps her clients improve communication, leadership and customer service skills, strengthen their commitment to multicultural inclusion and align their people-focused programs with their strategic business priorities.

As an author and consultant Tracy has made appearances on many local radio and television programs. She's also been interviewed or featured nationally in Money Magazine, BLR Reports, The Network Journal, HR Insights, Texas Business Monthly, HR Magazine, Heart and Soul Magazine and other publications.

But Tracy is not all work and community service. Whatever city her business might take her to you can often find her relaxing at a rollerskating rink, or in the audience of a play or jazz concert.

To Order Additional Books

www.TheWayLeadersThink.com

Also available at www.amazon.com

LeaderThink® Volume 1   LeaderThink® Volume 2

LeaderThink® Email Newsletter

If you want to receive new LeaderThink® messages each Monday morning, subscribe to the email newsletter.

Send an email to: Leaderthink-Subscribe@tracybrown.com or Visit the website: www.TheWayLeadersThink.com and complete the subscription box.

Instructions for subscribing to the RSS feed are also on the website.

LeaderThink® Podcast
www.BlogTalkRadio.com/leaderthink

Listen or subscribe to the LEADERTHINK PODCAST to hear expanded versions of some of the most popular LeaderThink® messages!

Your Comments Are Welcome
If you have feedback about the book, let us know.

BY PHONE
Leave a voicemail toll-free (in the U.S.) by calling 1.800.290.5631.

BY EMAIL
Send your comments or questions to:
staff@TheWayLeadersThink.com

Made in the USA
Monee, IL
11 April 2025

15501812R00089